T0023856

DAD JOKES

To:

From:

Highlights

DAD JOKES

THE Cheesiest, Corniest JOKE BOOK EVER!

KID TESTED BY:
Luke & Levi
AGES 7 & 4
with their dad, Seth

Highlights Press
Honesdale, Pennsylvania

Contributing Illustrators: David Arumi, Lee Cosgrove, David Coulson, Mike Dammer, Briana Dengoue, Keith Frawley, Kelly Kennedy, Pat Lewis, Rich Powell, Kevin Rechin, Rick Stromoski, Brian Michael Weaver, Brian White, Pete Whitehead, Kevin Zimmer

Copyright © 2024 by Highlights for Children
All rights reserved.
Copying or digitizing this book for storage, display or distribution in any other medium is strictly prohibited.

For information about permission to reprint selections from this book, please contact permissions@highlights.com.

Published by Highlights Press
815 Church Street
Honesdale, Pennsylvania 18431
ISBN: 978-1-63962-153-8
LCCN: 2023941662
Printed in Robbinsville, NJ
Mfg. 12/2023

First edition
Visit our website at Highlights.com.

10 9 8 7 6 5 4 3 2 1

Contents

Rise and Shine

What do you get when you cross a rooster and a duck?

A wake-up call at the quack of dawn.

Why didn't the detective get out of bed?

She wanted to stay under-covers.

Dad: There's something wrong with my shaving brush.
Dan: That's funny. It was all right yesterday when I painted my bike.

What does a musician brush his teeth with?

A tuba toothpaste.

How does a caterpillar start its day?

It turns over a new leaf.

Jack: Time to get up, Grandad. It's five to eight.
Grandad: Who's winning?

What did the molecule's stepdad say to him every morning?

"Up and atom!"

What is an English teacher's favorite breakfast?

Synonym rolls.

Why was the traffic light late to work?

It took too long to change.

Camila: How do you take your coffee?
Dad: Seriously. Very seriously.

If the early bird gets the worm, I'll sleep in until there's pancakes.

Melissa: Dad, can you make me a breakfast sandwich?
Dad: *Poof!* You're a breakfast sandwich!

Rowan: You know that alarm clock Yéyé gave me?
Zoey: Yes.
Rowan: I had to take it back. It kept waking me up when I was sleeping.

Knock, knock.
Who's there?
Pudding.
Pudding who?
Pudding on your shoes before your pants is a bad idea.

What do ghosts wash their hair with?

Sham-boo.

Why was the broom late for school?

It over-swept.

Why did dad's coffee taste like mud?

Because it was fresh ground.

Papa, how do I look?

With your eyes.

Dad: Which sock are you looking for?
Grace: My missing ocean sock.
Dad: We're running late.
Just pick any sock.
Grace: But, Dad, I'm looking
for a Pacific sock.

Dad: I didn't have time to go jogging this morning.

Talia: You say that every day.

Dad: I know. It's a running joke.

What did the painter say when she got up in the morning?

"Good Monet!"

Patient: Every time I drink a cup of coffee, I get a sharp pain in my eye. What should I do?

Doctor: Just take the spoon out of your cup.

Why did the boy only put on one snow boot?

There was only a 50 percent chance of snow.

What did Dad say to his coffee cup?

"Words cannot espresso how much you mean to me."

What did the monster say to his father when he slept through his alarm?

"Sorry, I ogre-slept!"

Papi: Mira, did you make your bed today?
Mira: Yes, Papi, but I think it would be better to buy one.

What does a ghost have in his morning coffee?

Scream and sugar.

Dad, there's something in my shoe.

It's called your foot.

Aminah: My shoes don't fit right.
Dad: That's because you have them on the wrong feet.
Aminah: But these are the only feet I have!

What do aliens have for breakfast?

Flying sausages.

Around the House

What did the papa broom say to the baby broom?

"It's time to go to sweep."

Shayla: Hey, Dad! I got a haircut today.
Dad: Which one?

What time is it when the clock strikes 13?

Time to fix the clock.

Dad: Didn't I tell you to drink your medicine after your bath?
Ivy: But I didn't have any room after I drank my bath.

Daddy, can you put the dog out?

I didn't know it was on fire!

How does a banana answer the phone?

"Yellow!"

What would you be if you mixed your dad's red paint with black paint?

In trouble.

Knock, knock.
Who's there?
Rufus.
Rufus who?
Rufus leaking. You'd better get it fixed!

Dad: Did you give your fish fresh water?
Kelsey: No. He hasn't finished the water I gave him yesterday.

What's the difference between a television and a magazine?

Ever try swatting a fly with a television?

Where is a cat when the lights go out?

In the dark.

Dad: Remember to put your shoes on the right feet today.

Robin: But I only have one right foot.

Dad: What was that loud noise?

Hari: My jacket fell on the floor.

Dad: Why would your jacket falling make such a loud noise?

Hari: Because I was wearing it.

Why is it hard to eat a clock?

It's so time-consuming.

Dad: Why didn't you play school with your sister?
Jake: I did. I played I was absent.

If a red house is made out of red bricks and a blue house is made out of blue bricks, what is a greenhouse made out of?

Glass.

My dad asked if I could clear the table. I needed a running start, but I made it.

Dad: I feel like our first president.
Julian: What do you mean?
Dad: I'm Washing-a-ton of laundry!

Alex: Pa, would you ever scold me for something I didn't do?
Pa: Of course I wouldn't. Why do you ask?
Alex: I was just wondering because I didn't clean my room.

Josiah: Hey, Dad, the computer keeps crashing. What should I do?
Dad: Stop dropping it!

What amazing invention allows you to see through walls?

Windows.

Julia: Poppy! There's a monster under my bed!

Poppy: Tell it to get back in the closet where it belongs.

What does a cow use to cut the grass?

A lawn moo-er.

Kai: Poppa, may I call Jessi?

Poppa: Sure. Do you have her phone number?

Kai: No. That's why I need to call her.

What did the top hat say to the tie?

"You hang around, I'll go on ahead."

What do you call a lazy kangaroo?

A pouch potato.

Scientists have discovered what is believed to be the world's largest bedsheet. More on this story as it unfolds.

Dad: Jamar, you've lost your two front teeth.
Jamar: Oh, no, I haven't. I have them in my pocket.

Why did Dad sell the vacuum cleaner?

It was just gathering dust.

Dad: What was that big crash?
Zaid: You know that lamp you were worried I'd break?
Dad: Yes, I remember.
Zaid: Well, your worries are over.

Where's the best place to go at night?

To sleep.

Why did the kid put a ruler next to their bed?

Because they wanted to see how long they slept.

Pops, did you just take a shower?

Why, is there one missing?

Dad: What are you doing?
Jude: I'm washing my hands.
Dad: Without soap and water?
Jude: Haven't you heard of dry cleaning?

What's the loudest pet you can get?

A trumpet.

Dad: Get me a pencil and paper.
Ali: Why?
Dad: I'm going to draw you a bath.

A book just fell on my head.
I only have my shelf to blame.

What did the space rock say when his son came home caked with mud?

"Take a meteor shower."

Dad: Why didn't you pick up your room as I asked you to?

Stella: Because it was way too heavy.

What do you get if you give a dinosaur a pogo stick?

Big holes in your driveway.

Atul: Why did you throw away your dad's guitar?

Avery: Because it has a hole in the middle.

What did the sink say to the dishwasher?

"Get a load of this!"

Shull: Where are you going? Bumpa said not to walk on the kitchen floor unless your feet are clean.

Eyal: My feet are clean. It's my shoes that are dirty.

Megan: I have a problem.

Killian: What is it?

Megan: I have a room with yellow polka dots!

Killian: Why's that a problem?

Megan: My dad said my room has to be spotless!

I don't trust stairs. They are always up to something.

What did the washer say to the dryer?

"Let's go for a spin."

Knock, knock.
Who's there?
Dishes.
Dishes who?
Dishes not the last of my jokes!

What starts with *T*, ends with *T*, and is full of *T*?

A teapot.

What did the picture say to the wall?

"I've been framed!"

What do you call a lawyer's house?

A legal pad.

Why should you knock before opening the refrigerator?

Because you might see the salad dressing.

Kali: Dad, you're wearing one blue sock and one white sock.
Dad: That's funny. I saw another pair just like this one in my drawer.

How do you know when your dog has gotten into paint?

There are blueprints all over your house.

I've given my cactus plant-y of water and food, but it's one prickly eater.

Piano tuner: I'm here to tune your piano.
Lacy: I didn't call for a piano tuner.
Piano tuner: I know. Your dad did.

What animal can jump higher than a house?

All of them—houses can't jump.

Where do geologists like to relax?

In rocking chairs.

Fernanda: Last night, the people upstairs were stomping on the floor until after midnight.
Antonia: Did they keep you up?
Fernanda: Luckily, I was still awake practicing my tuba.

What do you do if you find a yak in your bed?

Sleep on the couch.

Have you heard the joke about the bed?

It hasn't been made yet.

That's a pretty good ceiling.
It's not the best, but it's up there!

Why was the girl punching her pillow?

Her grandpa said that he falls asleep as soon as he hits the pillow.

How does a penguin build its house?

Igloos it together.

Where does Santa keep his suit?

In the Claus-et.

Ren: Dad, I can't.
Dad: Ren, never say you can't do something.
Ren: Okay. Then will you please help me put the toothpaste back in the tube?

Hi, Hungry— I'm Dad!

Amelia: Are we having burgers on the grill?

Dad: No, I think they would be better on plates!

Dad: Jace, don't eat soup wearing a costume.

Jace: The soup isn't wearing a costume. I am!

How do you make a hot dog stand?

You take away its chair.

What happens when you leave alphabet soup on the stove?

It could spell disaster.

What do baseball players say when they're hungry?

"Butter up!"

Dad: What happened to all the cookies?
Leif: I didn't touch one of them.
Dad: But there's only one left.
Leif: That's the one I didn't touch.

Why was the cheddar yawning?

It was on a cheese bored.

What do daddy spices say to their kids on graduation day?

"Where did the thyme go?"

Elijah: Dad, these latkes taste kind of funny.
Dad: Then why aren't you laughing?

When should you avoid drinking a hot beverage?

When it's not your cup of tea.

Knock, knock.
Who's there?
Mister E.
Mister E. who?
Mister E. meat is what
Dad's making for dinner.

What did the ear of corn say when it was about to be peeled?

"Shucks."

Eat your spinach, son. It will put color in your cheeks.

But I don't want green cheeks, Papa!

Sophia: Hey, Dad. There's no bacon left!
Dad: Sorry, I guess I hogged it all.

What do you call a turtle chef?

A slow cooker.

What are two things you can't have for breakfast?

Lunch and dinner.

What do penguins order at Mexican restaurants?

Brr-ritos.

Dad: Would you like fish for dinner?
Enrique: I'm not into fish.
Dad: No, the fish goes into you.

What did the butter say as it was being spread?

"I'm on a roll!"

Why did dinosaurs drink cold tea?

Because fire wasn't discovered yet.

Why did the monster try to eat a light bulb?

It wanted a light snack.

Why was the oatmeal sad?

No raisin.

Knock, knock.
Who's there?
Fajita.
Fajita who?
Fajita another thing, I'll be stuffed.

How do you make a hamburger laugh?

You pickle it!

Dad: Jasmine, how many bowls of cereal have you eaten?
Jasmine: Just one. I filled it up five times.

How can you tell a chili bean from any other kind of bean?

It's the one wearing a sweater.

Chloe: Here, Dad, try some of my sponge cake.
Dad: It's a bit tough.
Chloe: I don't understand! I used a really fresh sponge.

Eleanor: Dad, you know bugs, right?
Dad: Yes, but let's not talk about bugs at dinner.
(10 minutes later)
Dad: Now that dinner's done, what was that about bugs?
Eleanor: Oh, I saw one in your salad, but it's gone now.

What did the hamburger name its daughter?

Patty.

Maile: Dad, I'm hungry.
Dad: Hi, Hungry. I'm Dad.
Maile: Dad, I'm serious!
Dad: I thought you were Hungry?

How do clowns like their eggs?

Funny-side up.

Did you hear what happened when the cheese factory blew up?

Da brie was everywhere.

What did the daddy lollipop ask the baby lollipop?

"Will you do me a big flavor?"

Why should you stare at the orange juice container?

It says concentrate.

What did the chicken finger's mom say when he got embarrassed?

"Fry not to blush."

Knock, knock.
Who's there?
Jupiter.
Jupiter who?
Jupiter fly in my soup?

What do you get when you eat two-thirds of a pie?

An upset stomach.

Why did the cookie cry?

His dad had been a wafer so long.

Makayla: Why is there an egg on the front porch and an egg on the back patio?
Ruth: My stepdad said to separate two eggs for the cake.

What did one burrito say to the other?

"Don't spill the beans!"

What do you use to fix a broken pizza?

Tomato paste.

What's the difference between a potato and an onion?

No one cries when you cut up a potato.

One day, a T. rex got tired of eating plants all the time. He turned to his friend and said, "I think becoming an herbivore was a missed steak."

Father: Do you want any more ABC soup?
Lilliana: No, thanks. I couldn't eat another syllable.

What did one plate say to the other?

"Lunch is on me today!"

What do you call leftover french fries?

Later taters.

Dad: Why did you throw your toast?
Lina: I wanted to see the butterfly!

First astronaut: What's that thing in the frying pan?
Second astronaut: It's an unidentified frying object.

What did the baby corn say to the mama corn?

"Where's popcorn?"

What do cheetahs like to eat?

Fast food.

Ivan: Dad, what's this fly doing in my ice cream?

Dad: Probably learning how to ski.

Where does spaghetti go to dance?

The meatball.

When should you keep an eye on your cheese?

When it's up to no Gouda.

Dad: Would you like an apple?
Clara: I don't feel like an apple today.
Dad: That's good. You don't look like an apple either.

What does a camera have for lunch?

Cheese.

Mary Poppins ordered cauliflower with cheese and four hard-boiled eggs at her favorite restaurant. After dinner, she wrote a review: Supercauliflowercheesebuteggswerequiteatrocious.

What cheese is made backward?

Edam.

First astronaut: Get ready for launch.
Second astronaut: But I haven't even had breakfast yet.

What did the bread say when it got in trouble?

"I'm toast!"

Knock, knock.
Who's there?
Ice-cream soda.
Ice-cream soda who?
**ICE-CREAM SODA WHOLE
WORLD CAN HEAR ME!**

Did you hear the joke about pizza?

Never mind. It's too cheesy.

Levi: Do you want the right half of this cupcake?
Dad: Sure— I certainly don't want the wrong half!

What's the best thing to put in a cookie?

Your teeth.

What did dinosaurs use to make hot dogs?

Jurassic pork.

Perfectly Punny

How do electric eels taste?

Absolutely shocking!

What do you call a belt with a clock on it?

A waist of time.

What's the best thing about Switzerland?

I don't know, but their flag is a huge plus.

What did the bald man say when he got a new comb?

"I shall never part with this."

What was the most groundbreaking invention of all time?

The shovel.

What do you call a fake noodle?

An im-pasta.

You may have noticed that I love silly puns. That's just how eye roll.

When is a door not a door?

When it's a jar.

Why did the cow cross the road?

To get to the udder side.

What is the opposite of bologna?

Above knee.

What's another name for a grandfather clock?

An old-timer.

Do you want to hear a paper joke?

Sorry, it's tear-ible.

What did summer say to spring?

"Help! I'm going to fall!"

Cup: Are you playing in the baseball game tomorrow?
Jug: I don't play baseball.
Cup: Oh, I thought you were a pitcher!

I once starred in a show about puns. It was a play on words.

Why did the farmer call the plumber?

To fix the leeks.

What are the two strongest days of the week?

Saturday and Sunday. The rest of them are weekdays.

Why did the phone wear glasses?

Because it lost all of its contacts.

What's the opposite of irony?

Wrinkly.

What's more amazing than a talking dog?

A spelling bee.

When does a joke become a dad joke?

When the punch line is apparent.

What do you call a moose with no name?

Anony-moose.

What happens if you're trying to drum but you don't know how?

Beats me!

I was confused when my printer started playing music until I realized the paper was jamming.

How does Dad get his coffee?

By whatever beans necessary.

What did one eye say to the other?

"Just between the two of us, there's something that smells."

What did the banana say to the ice cream?

"Let's split!"

Have you heard about the guy whose left side fell off?

He's all right now!

What's the difference between a fish and a piano?

You can't tuna fish.

Emma: I'm thirsty.
Dad: Hi, Thirsty. I'm Friday. Come over Saturday and we'll have a sundae!

Thanks for explaining the word many to me. It means a lot.

Why did the bacon laugh?

Because the egg told a funny yolk.

Knock, knock.
Who's there?
Offense.
Offense who?
**Offense has a hole in it—
better get it fixed!**

What did the palm tree say when it found out about chocolate-covered almonds?

"That's cocoa-nuts!"

What's brown and sticky?

A stick.

What do you call an alligator in a vest?

An investigator.

What did Mozart's dad say to him when he was misbehaving?

"Compose yourself!"

Why was the mummy upset?

She made a grave error.

Why did the shark spit out the clown?

Because she tasted funny.

Dad: Do you like your homework?
Nessa: I like *nothing* better.

Knock, knock.
Who's there?
Pecan.
Pecan who?
Pecan somebody your own size!

How far is it from March to June?

Just a short spring.

Knock, knock.
Who's there?
Falafel.
Falafel who?
Falafel my bike and hurt my knee.

What do you call a camel with no hump?

Humphrey.

Why was the baby pepper shaking?

It was a little chili.

Where do generals hide their armies?

In their sleevies.

What do you give a sick lemon?

Lemon aid.

What did Tennessee?

The same thing that Arkansas.

Out and About

What do you call a line of dads waiting to get haircuts?

A barber-queue.

Zara: Dad, where are you going?

Dad: I'm going jogging as soon as I stretch out my legs.

Zara: Why? Are they too short?

What did the buffalo say to his son when he dropped him off at school?

"Bye, son."

Judge: Order in the court!

Jury member: I'll have two cheeseburgers, please.

Clerk: That suit fits you like a glove.
Customer: Can you show me one that fits like a suit?

What would you do if an elephant sat in front of you at a movie?

Miss most of the film.

Latoya: Dad, I saw a dog as big as a house today!
Dad: Latoya, you know I've told you a million, billion, trillion times not to exaggerate.

A man walked into a bank and asked the teller to check his balance. She pushed him.

Why did the banana go to the doctor?

Because it wasn't peeling well.

Aidan: I saw a man-eating shark in the aquarium!
Lydia: That's nothing. I saw a girl eating shrimp in the zoo restaurant.

Why do you have your coat on over your bathing suit?

Because the water might be cold!

Waiter: Do you want a box for your leftovers?
Dad: No, but I'll wrestle you for them.

What did the man with two left feet ask the shoe salesperson?

"Do you have any flip-flips?"

John: Can you take me to the park on Friday?
Dad: Sure, but if it rains on Friday, what will we do?
John: Go the day before.

What did the ambitious elevator say to its dad?

"Things are looking up."

Knock, knock.
Who's there?
Jester.
Jester who?
Jester minute—I'm trying to find my car keys.

What is a dentist's favorite game?

Tooth or dare.

What's black and white and black and white and black and white?

A zebra in a revolving door.

What happened when the red ship and blue ship collided at sea?

Their crews were marooned.

Why are police officers the strongest people in the world?

They can hold up traffic with just one hand.

Hannah: Pop, may I have forty thousand dollars?
Pop: Why?
Hannah: Because I want to go the movies.
Pop: Movies don't cost that much!
Hannah: Yes, but it's a drive-in movie, and I don't have a car.

What did the dad say to his son when they got to the barbershop?

"Hair we are!"

How do lighthouse keepers communicate?

With shine language.

What time is the best to go to the dentist?

Tooth hurt-y.

Why did the book go to the doctor?

Because it hurt its spine.

Nolan: Can we go to the pool?
Dad: Well, it deep-ends on if we finish our chores!

Why did the cookie go to the doctor?

It felt crumby.

Riley: It's so hot today. Could you tell me a ghost story?
Dad: Sure, but why?
Riley: Because ghost stories are so chilling.

Cashier: Would you like the milk in a bag, sir?
Dad: No, just leave it in the carton!

What has more letters than the alphabet?

The post office.

Harper: Please throw your five fattest fish in the air.
Fish seller: Why?
Harper: So I can honestly tell my dad I caught them.

What do you call an elephant in a phone booth?

Stuck.

Knock, knock.
Who's there?
Alaska.
Alaska who?
**Alaska my dad if I can
come out and play.**

How many feet are in a mile?

*It depends on how many people are running
that mile.*

The other day, I was standing
in the park wondering why a
ball gets bigger and bigger the
closer it gets. Then it hit me!

**Why did the comedian wear a suit of armor to the
comedy show?**

To protect himself from the punch lines.

Why did the triangle jog around the block?

To get into shape.

What building has the most stories?

The library.

What did the judge say when a skunk walked into the courtroom?

"Odor in the court!"

Duck: I want to buy some lip balm.
Clerk: Will that be cash or charge?
Duck: Just put it on my bill.

Monster #1: We must be getting close to a city.
Monster #2: How can you tell?
Monster #1: We're stepping on more cars.

Yan: I'd like to buy a winter coat for my dad.
Clerk: How long would you like it?
Yan: He'll probably need it all winter.

What time is it when a giraffe steals your hat?

Time to get a new hat.

Customer: Waiter, is there any soup on the menu?
Waiter: No. I just wiped it off.

Two dinosaurs walked into a building. You'd think one of them would have seen it.

Diner: Do you serve crabs here?
Waiter: We serve anybody! Please sit down.

Shopper: Can I put this wallpaper on myself?
Store clerk: If you want, but it would look better on the wall.

Anika: Daddy, can you name five of these birds?
Daddy: Sure! How about Ariel, Diego, Eleni, Marta, and Dylan?

What did the poppa rock say when his son was scared to jump in the water?

"Don't be afraid to be a little boulder."

All in a Day's Work

What did the drummer call his twin daughters?

Anna One, Anna Two.

Caleb: My dad can't decide whether to get a cow or a bicycle for his farm.
Tia: He'd look silly riding around on a cow.
Caleb: Yeah, but he'd look a lot sillier trying to milk a bicycle.

Why was the computer late to work?

It had a hard drive.

Dad: How were the exam questions?
Logan: Easy. It was the answers that were tough!

Why did the mattress store employee get in trouble?

She was sleeping on the job.

Why do barbers always arrive first?

They know all the shortcuts.

Bone: I've been asked to be in a movie.
Body: Did you say yes?
Bone: No way! Who wants to be in a cast?

I used to have a job crushing pop cans. It was soda-pressing.

What's the secret to a good elevator pitch?

It has to work on many levels.

Dad, I got a B on my science test.

I hope it doesn't sting you.

What did the janitor say when he jumped out of the closet?

"Supplies!"

How did the rocket lose its job?

It got fired.

Why did the boy bring his grandad's credit card to school?

He wanted extra credit.

Teacher: We will have a half-day of school this morning.
Students: Hurray! Yippee!
Teacher: We will have the other half this afternoon.

Patrick: Dad, Mr. Crawford gave me an F for this drawing.

Dad: He did? That's a great drawing! Why would he give you an F?

Patrick: Because I drew it in French class.

What do you get when you cross a dog and an elephant?

A very nervous mail carrier.

Allison: My dad works in a clock factory.

Andrew: What does he do?

Allison: He stands around all day and makes faces.

What do you need to know if you're going to be a lion tamer?

More than the lion.

Where do walls meet after work?

The corner.

A rancher had 196 cows in her field, but when she rounded them up, she had 200.

Why did the dad have to go to school?

To take his pop quiz.

Micah: School is so confusing!
Dad: Why?
Micah: Ms. Rodriguez said, "One plus nine equals ten, six plus four equals ten, and seven plus three equals ten."
Dad: So?
Micah: She won't make up her mind!

Why were the scientists' heads wet?

They had a brainstorm.

What did the baker say when she won an award?

"It was a piece of cake."

Joelle: Papa, can you write your name in the dark?

Papa: I think so.

Joelle: Then would you turn off the lights and sign my report card?

Nora: I got a 100 in school today.

Dad: That's great! In what subject?

Nora: I got a 50 in spelling and a 50 in math.

Dad: What did you learn in school today?

Noah: Not enough. I have to go back tomorrow!

I refused to believe my dad was stealing from his job as a road worker, but when I got home all the signs were there.

What did the lawyer say when he shut his briefcase?

"Case closed!"

How many mystery writers does it take to change a light bulb?

Two. One to screw it in almost all the way, and one to give it a surprise twist at the end.

What did the ghost teacher say to the class?

"Look at the board and I will go through it again."

Dad: How did you do on your history test?
Sam: Not so well. They asked me about stuff that happened before I was born!

Father: What did you learn in school today?

Dalia: My teacher taught us writing.

Father: What did you write?

Dalia: I don't know. She hasn't taught us reading yet.

What did the cook name his son?

Stu.

There are three kinds of mathematicians: Those who can count and those who can't.

Why does it take so long to write a lullaby?

It keeps putting you to sleep!

Why did the ballerina quit her job?

It was tutu hard.

Tate: My teacher says that I have to write more clearly.
Dad: That's a good idea.
Tate: No, it isn't. Then she'll know I can't spell.

What did the singer name his daughter?

Melody.

Agriculture student: I'd be surprised if you got ten pounds of apples from that tree.
Farmer: So would I. It's a pear tree.

Why did the invisible man turn down a job offer?

He couldn't see himself doing it.

I wanted to be a history teacher, but there's just no future in it.

Teacher: Beatriz, name two pronouns.
Beatriz: Who? Me?

What did the sun say to the moon?

"Looks like it's my night off."

Oscar: So, how's your job?
Writer: It's all write.
Chimney cleaner: It soots me.
Crane operator: It has its ups and downs.

Why could the artist cross the bridge whenever he wanted?

It was a drawbridge.

Librarian #1: Want to go to the movies on Saturday?
Librarian #2: Thanks, but my weekend is all booked.

Why did the scientist take the doorbell off his house?

He wanted to win the no-bell prize.

Why did the boy eat his homework?

His dad told him it was a piece of cake.

How many bricks did the mason need to finish the building?

Just the last one.

Why did the scarecrow get a promotion?

He was outstanding in his field.

Fun and Games

What did the glove say to the baseball?

"Catch you later!"

Why is the football stadium so hot after the game?

All the fans are gone!

What's a golfer's favorite letter?

T.

I went fishing once, and now I'm hooked.

Jasper: Why are you doing the backstroke?
Aria: I just had lunch, and I don't want to swim on a full stomach.

What is an insect's favorite sport?

Cricket.

Why is basketball the messiest sport?

Because you dribble all over the floor.

What can you serve but not eat?

A tennis ball.

What's the best part of a boxer's joke?

The punch line.

What is dinner's favorite sport?

Biscuit-ball.

Why is tennis such a loud sport?

The players raise a racket.

What did the ballerina do after she hurt her foot?

She called a toe truck.

What is a basketball player's favorite cheese?

Swish.

Why can't dalmatians play hide-and-seek?

They'll always be spotted.

What is the first thing a ball does when it stops rolling?

It looks round.

What do football champions put their cereal in?

Super bowls.

Knock, knock.
Who's there?
Pasta.
Pasta who?
Pasta ball—I'm open!

How do you turn a walk into a run?

Load the bases.

Why are you back from your baseball game so soon?

My coach told me to run home.

What does a snail riding on a turtle's back say?

"Woo-hoo!"

Why did the golfer wear two pairs of socks?

In case he got a hole-in-one.

What kind of bees are bad at football?

Fumble-bees.

What's a zombie's favorite part of a hockey game?

The zomb-oni.

Dad: How did you do in the football game today?
Jayden: I made a 92-yard run.
Dad: That's great!
Jayden: Not really. I didn't catch the guy I was chasing.

What do you call a fly with no wings?

A walk.

What did the two strings do in the race?

They tied.

Since I quit soccer, I've lost my goal in life.

What did the farmer get when he let the football team practice on his field?

Mashed potatoes.

Why did the orange stop rolling down the hill?

It ran out of juice.

What did the magician say to the fisherman?

"Pick a cod, any cod."

Chicken leg: Are you game
to cheer at the match today?

Steak: Sure thing—meat you there!

Why couldn't the sailors play cards?

Because they were standing on the deck.

Did you hear about the race between the
two giraffes?

It was neck and neck.

Christy: Ann, why are you crying?

Ann: My bowling ball is broken.

Christy: How do you know?

Ann: It has holes in it.

What do you call a yo-yo with no string?

A no-yo.

What do you call a pig that knows karate?

A pork chop.

Hudson: Are there any athletes in your family?

Scarlett: My brother has been swimming for five years.

Hudson: He must be pretty tired.

Why do frogs make good outfielders?

They never miss a fly.

What is the hardest part about skydiving?

The ground.

Why shouldn't you play games in a cemetery?

You might be in grave danger.

Camila: Dad, I can't find my baseball mitt.
Dad: Did you check the glove compartment?

What sport do ants play with elephants?

Squash.

Anja: I can tell you the score of the ball game before it starts.
Djuka: Well, what is it?
Anja: Nothing to nothing.

Why don't golfers drink coffee?

They're always carrying tees.

What happened to the racing snail when its shell flew off?

It became a bit sluggish.

What did the mustard say during the race?

"I'll try to ketchup!"

Get the Door Already!

Knock, knock.
Who's there?
Ear.
Ear who?
Ear you are, Dad!

Knock, knock.
Who's there?
Sofa.
Sofa who?
Sofa so good.

Knock, knock.
Who's there?
Cereal.
Cereal who?
Cereal pleasure to have you over.

Knock, knock.
Who's there?
Butter chicken.
Butter chicken who?
Butter chicken the oven—something's burning!

Knock, knock.
Who's there?
A parrot.
A parrot who?
A-parrot-ly I'm at the wrong door.

Knock, knock.
Who's there?
Wheelbarrow.
Wheelbarrow who?
Wheelbarrow some money
from my dad.

Knock, knock.
Who's there?
Moustache.
Moustache who?
I moustache you a question, but I'll shave it for later.

Knock, knock.
Who's there?
Whinny.
Whinny who?
Whinny gets home, you can ask him.

Knock, knock.
Who's there?
Stopwatch.
Stopwatch who?
**Stopwatch you're doing
and open the door.**

Knock, knock.
Who's there?
I am.
I am who?
You mean you don't remember who you are?

Knock, knock.
Who's there?
Beets.
Beets who?
Beets me!

Knock, knock.
Who's there?
Jaws.
Jaws who?
Jaws stopped by to see if you want to go swimming.

Knock, knock.
Who's there?
Potato.
Potato who?
Potatoes don't have last names, silly!

Knock, knock.
Who's there?
Tinkerbell.
Tinkerbell who?
Tinkerbell is out of order.

Knock, knock.
Who's there?
Yacht.
Yacht who?
Yacht to know me by now!

Knock, knock.
Who's there?
Cheese.
Cheese who?
Cheese a very nice cat.

Knock, knock.
Who's there?
Groan.
Groan who?
Groan-ups like jokes as much
as kids.

Knock, knock.
Who's there?
Me.
Me who?
You sure have a funny-sounding cat!

Knock, knock.
Who's there?
Wing.
Wing who?
Wing, wing, wing. Hello?

Knock, knock.
Who's there?
Hygiene.
Hygiene who?
Hygiene! What's new with you, Gene?

Knock, knock.
Who's there?
Jessie.
Jessie who?
Jessie that man over there?
That's my stepfather.

Knock, knock.
Who's there?
Wheat.
Wheat who?
Wheat here, I'll go get my dad.

Knock, knock.
Who's there?
Canoe.
Canoe who?
Canoe help me give the dog
a bath?

Knock, knock.
Who's there?
Bean.
Bean who?
Bean here for ages. What kept you?

Knock, knock.
Who's there?
Spell.
Spell who?
W-H-O.

Knock, knock.
Who's there?
Fitzwilliam.
Fitzwilliam who?
Fitzwilliam better than it fits me.

Knock, knock.
Who's there?
A little boy.
A little boy who?
A little boy who can't reach the doorbell.

Knock, knock.
Who's there?
Whale.
Whale who?
Whale, whale, whale. I see your door is locked again.

Knock, knock.
Who's there?
Pizza.
Pizza who?
Pizza the puzzle is missing.

Knock, knock.
Who's there?
Stepfather.
Stepfather who?
One stepfather and you'll be inside.

Knock, knock.
Who's there?
Waffle.
Waffle who?
Waffle lot of fireflies out tonight!

Knock, knock.
Who's there?
Peas.
Peas who?
Peas open the door.
It's so cold outside!

Knock, knock.
Who's there?
Fiona.
Fiona who?
Fiona lookout for Mama and Papa.

Knock, knock.
Who's there?
Little old lady.
Little old lady who?
Oh, I didn't know you could yodel!

Knock, knock.
Who's there?
Who's.
Who's who?
You're the dad and I'm the son!

Knock, knock.
Who's there?
Worm.
Worm who?
It's worm in here, right?

Knock, knock.
Who's there?
Heywood, Hugh, and Harry.
Heywood, Hugh, and Harry who?
Heywood Hugh Harry up and open the door?

Knock, knock.
Who's there?
Joe King.
Joe King who?
Nothing. I'm just Joe King.

Knock, knock.
Who's there?
Amazon.
Amazon who?
Amazon of a teacher. What does your father do?

Knock, knock.
Who's there?
Avenue.
Avenue who?
Avenue heard enough of these jokes?

Knock, knock.
Who's there?
Pickle.
Pickle who?
Pickle little flower for your father.

Are We There Yet?

What did the car wheels say after a long drive?

"We're tired out!"

How do 37 mathematicians fit on a bus with 36 seats?

They carry the one.

How did the ice-cream truck get a flat tire?

It was on a rocky road.

How do you get over a fear of speed bumps?

You slowly get over it.

I read that by law you must turn on your headlights when it's raining in Sweden, but how am I supposed to know when it's raining in Sweden?

Why did the chicken cross the road?

The light was green.

Why did the spider buy a sports car?

So he could take it out for a spin.

What do you get when two giraffes collide?

A gir-affic jam.

What did the jack say to the car on the side of the road?

"Can I give you a lift?"

What do you call a polar bear in Hawai'i?

Lost.

Sandra: Have you heard the joke about the airplane?
Shawn: No, I haven't.
Sandra: Ah, never mind. It's way over your head.

What happens when frogs park illegally?

They get toad.

The other day, a chocolate truck got in an accident and spilled pieces of chocolate all across the road. I would have been late to work, but I took the road less truffled.

What kind of books do cars read?

Autobiographies.

How do fleas travel from place to place?

By itch-hiking.

Where do crayons go on vacation?

Colorado.

Why can't a motorcycle stand up by itself?

Because it's two-tired.

What is the best thing to take into the desert?

A thirst aid kit.

Why do ships in Norway have barcodes on their sides?

So when they come into port, they can Scandinavian.

Knock, knock.
Who's there?
Carl.
Carl who?
Carl get you there faster than a bike.

What did the car say when it snowed?

"I'm glad I'm wearing a hood."

Mountains really are the funniest place to travel. They're just hill areas.

What kind of food has cars and trucks in it?

Traffic jam.

What can go for miles and yet doesn't even move?

A road.

Why is an island like the letter *T* ?

It's in the middle of water.

What sound does a witch's car make?

Broom, broom!

What kind of car has whiskers and purrs?

A cat-illac.

What happened to the wooden car with the wooden wheels and the wooden engine?

It wooden go.

Andy: Have you seen the new train website?
Mylo: Yes—it's just the ticket!

Where do comedians go on vacation?

Joke-lahoma.

Why did the truck go to the doctor?

It had the pickups.

Why did the man fix his car horn?

It didn't give a hoot.

What did the trapeze artist do on her vacation?

She really let go.

What do you call a lost wolf?

A where-wolf.

Why didn't the elephant carry a suitcase?

He already had a trunk.

Pretend you're in Africa and a cheetah is chasing you. What do you do?

Stop pretending!

I phoned the airline office and asked, "How long does it take to get to Boston?" The clerk said, "Just a minute." "Thanks!" I said and hung up.

What did the wheel say to the brake?

"Why did you stop? I was on a roll."

What do you call it when a giraffe swallows a toy jet?

A plane in the neck.

What happens when you wear a watch on a plane?

Time flies!

If you rowed a boat all day and didn't get anywhere, what did you forget?

To untie the boat.

Where does a hamster go on vacation?

Hamster-dam.

What do you call a truck full of bison?

A buffa-load.

What does a car become when it goes into the car wash?

Wet.

What kind of vehicle does an egg drive?

A Yolks-wagen.

What did the tire say to the driver?

"Give me a brake."

Why don't mummies like to take vacations?

They're afraid to relax and unwind.

Where do boats go when they get sick?

To the dock.

Knock, knock.
Who's there?
Tree.
Tree who?
Tree more days 'til vacation!

I had a dream that I was a muffler last night. When I woke up, I was exhausted.

How can you tell that a train just went by?

You can see its tracks.

What happened when the boy took the train home?

His papi made him bring it back.

What is a mushroom's favorite vacation spot?

Portabella.

What did the father ghost say to his children when they got into the car?

"Put on your sheet belts."

What did the bread do on vacation?

It loafed around.

What did the mommy car and daddy car call their baby-boy car?

Carson.

Dad: Why didn't you take the school bus home?

Jian: I tried, but it wouldn't fit in my backpack.

Jaxon and his parents were driving along the road when it started to rain. Jaxon's dad flipped a switch, and snakes started crawling across the window. "Don't worry," Jaxon's dad said. "Those are just the windshield vipers."

Knock, knock.
Who's there?
Alpaca.
Alpaca who?
Alpaca the trunk, you pack-a the suitcase.

Animal Antics

What did the porcupine say when it bumped into a cactus?

"Hi, Dad."

Why did the clam refuse to share?

It was shellfish.

What happened to the cat that swallowed a ball of yarn?

She had mittens.

What's louder than a whooping crane?

A trumpeting swan.

Why do tigers have stripes?

So they don't get spotted.

A woman was riding a horse through the woods when she passed a rabbit. "Good morning," said the rabbit. The woman rode a little farther, then said, "I didn't know rabbits could talk." "Neither did I," said her horse.

Lily: Pop Pop bought me a pet bird.
Luke: What kind?
Lily: A keet.
Luke: Don't you mean a parakeet?
Lily: No, he just bought me one.

What do you call a container full of ducks?

A box of quackers.

Why did the elephant stand on a marshmallow?

Because it didn't want to fall into the hot chocolate.

What is black and white and red all over?

A sunburned zebra.

What do kittens call their father?

Paw.

Pops: What's wrong, son?
Eddie: I lost my cat.
Pops: Don't cry. We'll put an ad in the paper.
Eddie: That won't help. The cat can't read.

Why did the calf drink his milk?

His dad said it was moo-*tricious.*

What do you say to a blue whale?

"Cheer up!"

When is a dog's tail not a dog's tail?

When it's a wagon.

Why do cows have bells?

Because their horns don't work.

Why couldn't the marsupial get a job?

It wasn't koala-fied.

Why did the pony go to the doctor?

She was a little horse.

How did the officiant start the cow's wedding?

"Dairy beloved . . ."

What did the dad chameleon say to his nervous kid on the first day of school?

"Don't worry, you'll blend right in!"

What did the baby pig call his father's brother?

His oink-*le.*

Mama owl: I am so worried about our son.
Papa owl: What is the matter with him?
Mama owl: He doesn't give a hoot about anything.

What do you call a cow after an earthquake?

A milkshake.

Dogs are not allowed to operate an MRI machine, but cats can!

How do birds start their morning exercises?

With a worm-up.

What instrument does a turkey play?

The drumsticks.

What do baby birds call their dad?

Feather.

What's the difference between an African rhino and an Indian rhino?

About three thousand miles.

What's the best way to communicate with a fish?

Drop it a line.

Will: Why do bears paint their faces yellow?

Wynnie: I don't know. Why?

Will: So they can hide in banana trees.

Wynnie: Impossible! I've never seen a bear in a banana tree.

Will: See? It works!

How can you tell alligators and crocodiles apart?

One will see you later, and the other will see you in a while.

Why did Mozart get rid of his chickens?

They kept saying "Bach, Bach, Bach."

What is more difficult than getting a hippo into a hammock?

Getting two hippos into a hammock.

Why shouldn't you trust a minnow?

It's a little fishy.

I asked a farmer how long cows should be milked. "About the same as short ones," he said.

Snake #1: Are we poisonous?
Snake #2: I don't know. Why?
Snake #1: I just bit my lip!

Why did the man take his dog to the railroad station?

To get him trained.

What's the difference between a fly and a bat?

A bat can fly, but a fly can't bat!

What do you call a gorilla wearing earmuffs?

It doesn't matter. He can't hear you.

What did the cat say after she teased another cat?

"I'm sorry I hurt your felines. I was just kitten."

How can you tell old rabbits from young rabbits?

Look for the gray hares.

What did the horse say when he got to the bottom of his feed bag?

"This is the last straw!"

Goran: Does a cow remind you of something?
Marija: No, but it does ring a bell.

What do you get when a chicken lays its eggs on top of a hill?

Eggrolls.

What do you call a pig that sat in the sun too long?

Bacon.

What's the difference between a horse and a duck?

One goes quick, and the other goes quack!

Two fish friends hadn't seen each other in a while. One day, they ran into each other. The first fish said to the second, "Long time no sea!"

What did the farmer say to the cows at night?

"It's pasture bedtime."

What's the hardest part of giving an elephant a bath?

Getting her into the tub.

What's stranger than seeing a catfish?

Seeing a fishbowl.

What do you call a whale that can't keep a secret?

A blubber-mouth.

If you find a rabbit eating your dictionary, what should you do?

Take the words right out if its mouth.

Gabriel: My dad just bought me a jay.

Wyatt: A blue jay?

Gabriel: No. It's a happy one.

What happened when the dog swallowed a firefly?

He barked with delight.

Why do bears sleep all winter?

Would you be brave enough to wake up a bear?

Papi, do deer have uncles?

No, they only have antlers.

What do you call a pile of cats?

A meow-tain.

What lives in the ocean and always agrees with you?

A seal of approval.

Why do seahorses only like salt water?

Because pepper water makes them sneeze.

How do you catch an elephant?

Hide in a bush and make a noise like a peanut.

What do you call an indecisive bee?

A maybe.

Why don't termites drink coffee?

It makes them jitterbugs.

Server: Mr. Bear, what would you like to eat?
Mr. Bear: A cheeseburger and some . . . fries.
Server: Why the big pause?
Mr. Bear: I don't know. I've always had big paws.

Why do birds fly south for the winter?

Because it's too far to walk.

Why was the father caterpillar upset?

Because all of his kids needed new shoes.

I bought a dog from a blacksmith today. As soon as we got home, it made a bolt for the door.

The Great Outdoors

What's worse than raining cats and dogs?

Hailing taxis.

What do you do if you're out on the ocean and a whale sneezes?

Put up your sail.

How do you fix a broken pumpkin?

With a pumpkin patch.

What did the banana say to the apple on a sunny summer day?

"Better go inside—you're red, and I'm already peeling!"

I put on my puffiest coat, hat, scarf, gloves, and boots to shovel the snow, but found out my neighbor already did it. I was all dressed up with snowhere to go.

Ethan: The weather forecast says there's some ferocious rain outside.
Dad: I'll say! Forget about cats and dogs—it's raining dinosaurs!

How do you know when the moon is done eating?

When it's full.

What happened when the jester fell in a pond?

He got joking wet.

Dallas: Dad, can I go out and play?
Dad: What? With that torn shirt?
Dallas: No, with the kid across the street.

Where do oak trees come from?

Oak-lahoma.

> Yesterday it was snowing and today it all melted. Icy come, icy go, I suppose.

What did one mountain say to the other mountain?

"Meet me in the valley."

Why did the sun go to school?

To get brighter.

What did the dad volcano say to the baby volcano?

"Don't erupt me while I'm talking."

Knock, knock.
Who's there?
Wet.
Wet who?
**Wet me in!
It's waining!**

What do you call three trees planted at the same time?

Tree-plets.

What should you do when it's raining cats and dogs?

Try to avoid stepping on a poodle.

What did the rock say to the grass?

Nothing. Rocks can't talk.

How do you find out the weather when you're on vacation?

Look out the window.

What did one volcano say to the other?

"Stop interrupting me!"

Why shouldn't you tell secrets in the garden?

The potatoes have eyes and the corn has ears.

What do you call a really big ant?

A giant.

How do you know when the moon is broke?

When it's down to its last quarter.

Zoey: Do you know why that willow is always surrounded by fog?
Pops: It's a mist tree to me.

Did I ever tell you the story of when I climbed Mount Everest? I made it up.

What do monsters put on when it's sunny out?

Sun-scream.

Dad, can you explain to me what a solar eclipse is?

No sun.

What are the clumsiest things in the galaxy?

Falling stars.

What do you call a dad playing in the snow with no coat?

A Popsicle.

What did the wood say to the fire?

"You crackle me up."

What do you call it when sandwiches fall down a mountain?

An ava-lunch.

What did one ocean say to the other?

Nothing—it just waved.

Did you hear about the camping trip?
It was in tents.

What do you call a mix of snow and rain?

Sleets me!

Why shouldn't you play hide-and-seek with mountains?

They always peak.

Dad: What are you doing up in the pecan tree?
Chloe: Nuttin'.

What did the beaver say to the tree?

"Nice gnawing you!"

What is it called when the sun and Earth chat?

A heat and greet.

Why did the singer climb up a mountain?

To reach the high notes.

What do you call a fake Irish stone?

A shamrock.

Knock, knock.
Who's there?
Geometry.
Geometry who?
Geometry in the nature play,
but I wish I were a flower.

Megara: Do you think we should swim here? I heard
there were crocodiles.
Peggy: Don't worry. The sharks scare them away.

Why is it bad to iron a four-leaf clover?

Because you should never press your luck.

What's the best way to make a fire with two sticks?

Make sure one stick is a match.

I don't trust trees. They're a little shady.

Dad: Oh, no! What happened?
Noah: You see that tree over there?
Dad: Yes.
Noah: Well, I didn't.

How do fireflies start a race?

"Ready, set, GLOW!"

How did the trendy squirrel end up in a lake?

He was ice-skating before it was cool.

How can you identify a dogwood tree?

By its bark.

What did one snowperson say to the other?

"Do you smell carrots?"

What do you call a seagull that lives by the bay?

A bay-gull.

What did the bee say to the flower?

"Hi, Bud!"

Dana: You know what bugs me about June?

Dad: What?

Dana: June bugs.

What do you call a snowman in the summer?

A puddle.

What wears a coat in the winter and pants in the summer?

A dog.

Plateaus are the highest form of flattery.

What did the tree say when spring came?

"What a re-leaf!"

Books Never Written by Dads

I Love Pizza
by Peppa Roney

Machinery
by Howet Works

The World of Construction
by Jack Hammer

Winning
by Lou Zing

Exciting Adventures
by I. M. Bored

Tasty Vegetables
by Sue Keeney

Falling Trees
by Tim Burr

How to Make a Movie
by Holly Wood

The Man Who Could Not Fall Asleep
by Eliza Wake

Check Your Homework
by R. U. Wright

How to Solve Mysteries
by I. Guess

Downpour
by Wayne Dwops

Eat Your Veggies
by Brock A. Lee

Use Charcoal to Grill
by Barb B. Cue

What Do April Showers Bring?
by Mei Flowers

To the Eye Doctor
by Ken U. See

Itchy Bugs
by Amos Keeto

Smart People
by Gene E. Us

How to Keep Fit
by Jim Nasium

Writing a Novel
by Paige Turner

How to Learn
by Rita Book

Bathing Your Cat
by Manny Scratches

How to Be Serious
by Joe King

Staring Contest
by Kent Blink

Calling the Plumber
by Russ T. Pipe

Who Stole the Cookies?
by Miss Terry

A History of Stuffed Animals
by Ted E. Bear

Great Breakfast Recipes
by Pam Cake

Long Way Home
by Juana Ride

How to Cook Pasta
by Lynne Guini

Beating the Clock
by Justin Time

Water Transportation
by Rowan Boats

Be Prepared
by Justin Case

Anatomy of a Shark
by Rosa Teeth

How to Be Nice
by Karen N. Sharon

Where to Sit in Class
by Wayne Front

A Thanksgiving Story
by Ada Lott

Running the Mile
by Otto Breath

The Perfect S'more
by Graham Cracker

Let's Celebrate!

What did the cat say at midnight on New Year's?

"Meow."

What can you throw but not catch?

A party.

What did the dad say at 12 a.m. on January 1?

"Man, I'm hungry. I haven't eaten all year!"

Every year, I look forward to an amazing New Year's celebration at Times Square, but they always drop the ball.

Dad: What do you want for your birthday?

Omar: I can't tell you, or it wouldn't be a surprise.

Did you hear about the elevator dance?

It has no steps.

Where do you find a present for a cat?

In a catalogue.

Why was it hard to plan Papaw's birthday?

He was very party-cular.

Why does Ramadan remind you of a history book?

There are many dates.

Why was the Easter bunny upset?

It was having a bad hare day.

Why shouldn't you tell an Easter egg a joke?

It might crack up.

Knock, knock.
Who's there?
Doughnut.
Doughnut who?
**Doughnut open this
until the bar mitzvah.**

What should you not say to matzo on Passover morning?

"Rise and shine."

Dad: Would you like a pocket calculator for your birthday?
Gavi: No, thanks. I already know how many pockets I have.

The wedding was so beautiful even the cake was in tiers.

Who did the deer invite to his party?

His nearest and deer-est friends.

Mateo: Did everyone like your piñata at your Cinco de Mayo party?
Marisol: It was a big hit!

Why do melons have weddings?

They cantaloupe.

Knock, knock.
Who's there?
Rabbit.
Rabbit who?
Rabbit carefully—
it's a present for my poppa.

What phrase do you use to start a parade?

"Let's get this show on the road!"

What kind of bagel should you serve on Father's Day?

Poppy seed.

Mushroom #1: Wow, you have so many party invitations.
Mushroom #2: Well, I'm a really fungi!

The past, the present, and the future walked into the party. It was tense.

What was the dad's favorite Father's Day gift?

The last two were a tie.

Knock, knock.
Who's there?
Butternut.
Butternut who?
Butternut forget your father's birthday!

How do you find out a dinosaur's age?

Go to its birthday party.

Why is a giraffe a bad party guest?

It eats, leaves.

What did the father pill say to the baby pill when the guests arrived?

"Aren't you going to vitamin?"

Michael: Do they have the Fourth of July in England?

Dad: Yes. They also have the second and third of July.

Zach: I once sang "The Star-Spangled Banner" for three hours nonstop.

Jack: That's nothing. I can sing "The Stars and Stripes Forever."

Where was the birthday candle born?

Wish-consin.

Knock, knock.
Who's there?
Bacon.
Bacon who?
Bacon a cake for your birthday!

What game do tornadoes play at parties?

Twister.

What is a clock's favorite birthday gift?

The present.

What does every birthday end with?

y!

Dad: Did you thank Ms. Rubin for hosting the party?
Beth: No, Dad. The girls leaving before me thanked her, and Ms. Rubin said, "Don't mention it," so I didn't.

Knock, knock.
Who's there?
Farmer.
Farmer who?
I want a dog farmer birthday.

How do construction workers party?

They raise the roof.

What did the house wear to the party?

Address.

Why didn't the skeleton go trick-or-treating?

It had no body to go with.

My son's fourth birthday was today. When I walked in his room, I didn't recognize him at first. I had never seen him be four.

Why did the police officer ticket the ghost on Halloween?

It didn't have a haunting license.

What is a boxer's favorite party drink?

Punch.

Did you hear about the zombie Halloween party?

It was a scream.

Why do we put candles on the top of a cake?

It's easier than putting them on the bottom.

How does a beluga celebrate its birthday?

With a whale of a party!

What did the salad say when it got to the party?

"Lettuce turnip the beet!"

How do cats bake a bat mitzvah cake?

From scratch.

What kind of music did the Pilgrims listen to on Thanksgiving?

Plymouth rock.

What did the dreidel say to the menorah?

"Spin too long since we saw each other."

How do you throw a party in outer space?

You planet.

What kind of bow can't you put on a present?

An elbow.

What happens if you eat Christmas decorations?

You get tinsel-itus.

What did the hedgehog say to the Christmas tree?

"Is that you, Dad?"

How did Sofia greet her father on Christmas morning?

"Feliz Navi-Dad!"

How can you tell if a hippo's been to your party?

Look for footprints in the ice cream.

Jada: My son came to visit for Kwanzaa.
Alexis: Nice! Did you meet him at the airport?
Jada: Oh, no. I've known him for years!

Why did the boy put a slice of bread in the oven at midnight on December 31?

He wanted to make a New Year's toast.

Why couldn't prehistoric people send holiday cards?

The stamps kept falling off the rocks.

Knock, knock.
Who's there?
Frankfurter.
Frankfurter who?
Frankfurter lovely present!

Knee
Slappers

What do you call a fish with no eyes?

A fsh.

Garrett: Dad, what does A-B-Z-Y-W-T-N-I-T spell?
Dad: Nothing.
Garrett: Wow! I never knew that's how you spell *nothing!*

How do you make seven even?

Take away the s.

Can February march?

No, but April may.

Knock, knock.
Who's there?
Tire.
Tire who?
Tire shoes before you trip.

What has five toes and isn't your foot?

My foot.

What do you do if you see a skeleton running across the road?

Jump out of your skin and join him!

Why did the chicken cross the road?

To get to the other side.

Why did the farmer cross the road?

To bring back his chicken.

Dad: I have good news, and I have bad news.
Brekken: What's the good news?
Dad: The good news is that there's no bad news.

What do you call it when it rains cats?

A down-purr.

Why did the vampire get in trouble with her dad?

Because she had a bat attitude.

Where does Friday come before Thursday?

In the dictionary.

Abigail: My dad is a magician who can saw people in half.

Mark: Do you have any brothers or sisters?

Abigail: Yes, I have four half sisters.

David's father had four kids. Their names were North, South, East, and what?

David.

Which president wore the biggest hat?

The one with the biggest head.

Derek: I'm feeling a little cold.

Dad: Go stand in the corner. It's 90 degrees!

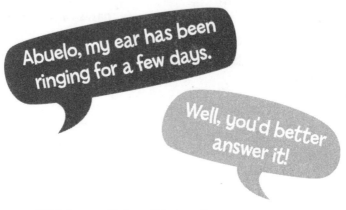

Abuelo, my ear has been ringing for a few days.

Well, you'd better answer it!

Which month has 28 days?

They all do.

Fern: Isaiah, do you know what D-A-D spells?
Isaiah: Yes.
Fern: No, it spells *dad*.

Theo: Hey, Dad, I know a lot about money.
Dad: How?
Theo: I have a head full of sense.

What dinosaur is a terrific father?

Tricera-pops

How do you hurt a joke?

By giving it a punch line.

What should you do if a teacher rolls her eyes at you?

Roll the eyes back to her.

Samuel: Daddy, I'm glad you named me Samuel.
Daddy: Why?
Samuel: Because that's what everyone calls me.

What do you call a boomerang that doesn't come back?

A stick.

Dad: If I had five coconuts and I gave you three, how many would I have left?

Nia: I don't know.

Dad: Why not?

Nia: In our school, we do arithmetic with apples and oranges.

What does it mean when you find a horseshoe?

Some horse is walking around in just socks.

Ezra: Did you ever see an egg roll?

Dad: No, but I've seen an apple turn over.

How do you stop a skunk from smelling?

You hold its nose.

What happens once in a month, twice in a moment, but never in a hundred years?

The letter M.

I had a date last night. It was perfect. Tomorrow, I'll have a grape.

Do you want to hear a construction joke?

I'm still working on it.

What kind of shoes do spies wear?

Sneakers.

Mariah: Can you telephone from a space shuttle?
Molly: Of course I can tell a phone from a space shuttle!

What's white, black, and blue all over?

A ghost that can't go through walls.

Knock, knock.
Who's there?
Ketchup.
Ketchup who?
Ketchup with me and you'll find out.

What do you do with a green monster?

Wait until it ripens.

Where was the Declaration of Independence signed?

At the bottom.

What's black and white and has sixteen wheels?

A dalmatian on roller skates.

What's the easiest way to catch a fish?

Have somebody throw it to you.

What did the cheese say when it got its picture taken?

"People!"

Why do books make great police officers?

They're undercover.

If you have five apples in one hand and five jars of honey in the other hand, what do you have?

Big hands.

Why does a flamingo stand on one leg?

Because if it lifted both legs, it would fall over!

Hilarious Hobbies

What's the best place to eat while hiking?

A fork in the road.

Hey, Dad. What's this movie about?

It's about two hours.

Waylon: Daddy, what are those holes in the wood?
Dad: Those are knotholes.
Waylon: But if they're not holes, what are they?

Why do pandas like old movies?

Because they're in black and white.

What do you drink before a marathon?

Lots of running water.

Where do you learn to make banana splits?

In sundae school.

I used to play the piano by ear, but now I use my hands.

What kind of bikes do fathers ride?

Pop-cycles.

Why do gardeners hate weeds?

If you give them an inch, they'll take a yard.

What do mice wear to play basketball?

Squeakers.

Why did the dad keep buying books for his library?

He had no shelf control.

I like doing push-ups. Hands down, they're my favorite exercise.

Knock, knock.
Who's there?
Arkansas.
Arkansas who?
Arkansas through any piece of wood in less than ten seconds!

What did the astronaut read in space?

Comet books.

What did the lonely checkerboard say?

"I'm board."

212

In what sport do you sit down going up and stand up going down?

Snowboarding.

Man #1: Excuse me, sir, but do you see that sign? It says "No Fishing Allowed."
Man #2: Oh, I'm not fishing aloud—I'm fishing very quietly.

What's the difference between wearing a tux on a bicycle and wearing a sports jersey on a unicycle?

Attire.

What's green and sings?

Elvis Parsley.

Why are cats good at video games?

They all have nine lives.

What's a tortilla chip's favorite dance?

Salsa.

What's the best kind of book to read when you're sick?

Sinus fiction.

What do you call a dog magician?

A lab-racadabrador.

What do you get when you cross a science-fiction film with a toad?

Star Warts.

Kari: I can't put this model airplane together.
Dad: But the directions say that a five-year-old can do it.
Kari: No wonder. I'm eleven.

When is a blue book not a blue book?

When it is read.

The hills are alive...

What is a cow's favorite musical?

The Sound of Moo-sic.

How do you watch movies in a haunted house?

On a big-scream TV.

Why did the robot go on vacation?

To recharge his batteries.

How does a lion paddle a canoe?

He uses his roar.

Fisherman #1: I'd like to catch something shiny and expensive.
Fisherman #2: How about a goldfish?

What do you call a friend that doesn't let you play a video game?

A control freak.

I've been bored recently, so I decided to take up fencing. The neighbors keep demanding that I put it back.

How did the egg get up the mountain?

It scrambled up.

Why did the monster's pop knit him another sock?

He heard he grew another foot.

Who writes books about haunted houses?

Ghostwriters.

What kind of garden does a baker have?

A flour garden.

oh! oh! oh!

Who says "Oh, oh, oh"?

Santa skiing backward.

Knock, knock.
Who's there?
Halibut.
Halibut who?
Halibut we go to the movies tonight?

What kind of music should you listen to while fishing?

Something catchy!

Where do cats go to look at art?

The meow-seum.

What kind of scenes do sheep like to paint?

Lamb-scapes.

Why did the dad stop making doughnuts?

He got tired of the hole business.

After many years, I decided to take up my novel project again. It was a move in the write direction.

What do you call a funny golf ball?

A goof ball.

Why can't pine trees knit?

They're always dropping their needles.

What did the guitar say to the musician?

"Stop picking on me!"

I tried to learn the physics of juggling, but it's all over my head.

Witty One-Liners

I tell dad jokes.
Sometimes he laughs.

Yesterday, I was washing the car with my son. He said, "Dad, can't you just use a sponge?"

My sister challenged me to build a race car out of spaghetti. You should have seen her face when I sped pasta.

Did you know that the first french fries weren't cooked in France? They were cooked in Greece.

I used to hate facial hair, but then it started growing on me.

Sundays can be sad, but the day before is a sadder day.

I was thinking about investing in duct tape, but I was worried it would be a rip-off.

I thought I'd like decorations
on the front door, but now I'm really
wreath-inking my decision.

Did you hear about the boatbuilder who had to start
working from home? His sails went through the roof.

I'm so good at sleeping that I do it with my
eyes closed.

After a perfect birthday spent with everyone I love, my son whipped up a batch of his famous chocolate frosting. That was just the icing on the cake.

I'm terrified of elevators. I'm going to take steps to avoid them.

My puppy has been sick all week, and this morning she had a fever. I gave her some mustard. I've heard that's the best thing for a hot dog.

I'm reading a book about antigravity. It's impossible to put down!

I would tell you a chemistry joke, but I don't think it would get a reaction.

I try not to check out too many library books at a time. I don't want to overdue it.

The witch claimed she was looking for a new job, but she was just going through the potions.

Pops asked me to put ketchup on the grocery list. Now I can't see anything.

I wanted to be a doctor. I just didn't have the patients.

I bought a new sleeping bag last month. I've spent the past four weeks trying to wake it up.

I have a condition that makes me eat when I can't sleep. It's called insom-nom-nom-nom-nia.

Did you hear about the new restaurant in space? The food was good, but there was no atmosphere.

A business executive's work bag went missing yesterday. The detectives already found it. It was a brief case.

Someone glued my deck of cards together. I don't know how to deal with it.

Time flies like an arrow. Fruit flies like a banana.

A sign on the escalator said Dogs Must Be Carried. I spent the next two hours looking for a dog.

Two goldfish were in a tank. One goldfish said to the other, "Do you know how to drive this thing?"

Singing in the shower is fun until you get soap in your mouth. Then it becomes a soap opera.

I gave all my dead batteries away today free of charge.

I saw a guy fighting with a scarecrow the other day. I thought, "He's just clutching at straws."

I was making shelves for a bookcase and accidentally cut one too short. I guess it's back to the sawing board.

I've got a pen that can write underwater. It can write other words, too, but underwater is one of my favorites.

I told my dad he shouldn't burn his old papers from school, but he did it anyway. He was just adding fuel to the fire.

I tried to catch some fog yesterday, but I mist.

There's a difference between bad jokes and dad jokes. That difference is the first letter.

If someone in the desert tells you they're thirsty, give them the benefit of the drought.

I wanted to grow herbs in my garden, but I couldn't find the thyme.

Two frogs were sitting on a lily pad,
eating lunch. One said to the other,
"Time sure is fun when you're having flies. "

I used to work at a clothing manufacturer. One day, a group of customers was pretty rude, but I decided to cut them some slacks.

My friend said something funny about invisibility. If only I could see the joke.

Scientists recently managed to weigh a rainbow. Turns out it was pretty light.

I once wrote a song about a tortilla, but it's more of a wrap.

Apparently you can't use *beefstew* as a password. It's not stroganoff.

Gravity jokes are getting old, but I fall for them every time.

Do birds know where they are going
when they fly south for the winter,
or are they just winging it?

I've stayed up three nights trying to come up with the
perfect mountain pun. I don't know if I'll Everest.

To the person who invented zero: thanks
for nothing!

I've started sleeping in our fireplace. Now I'm sleeping like
a log!

I didn't think my pancakes would be that popular, but they're selling like hotcakes.

I only know 25 letters of the alphabet. I don't know y.

Waking up this morning was an eye-opening experience.

The rotation of Earth really makes my day.

I was going to tell you a time-traveling joke, but you didn't like it.

You know, I never used to like "The Hokey Pokey," but then I turned myself around.

A sheep, a drum, and a snake fall down a hill. Ba-dum-TSS!

Whoever said that words will never hurt you has never been hit in the head with a dictionary.

I
Lava
You

What did the koala give his dad for Father's Day?

A bear hug.

What was the baby computer's first word?

"Data!"

Ruth: Dad, I have jelly on my face.
Dad: Well, wash it off. You're already sweet enough without it.

Knock, knock.
Who's there?
Kentucky.
Kentucky who?
Dad Kentucky you in at night.

What did the calculator say to the student?

"You can count on me."

Will you remember me in a year?

Yes.

Will you remember me in a month?

Yes.

Will you remember me in a week?

Yes.

Knock, knock.

Who's there?

See? You forgot me already!

Dad—it sounds cheesy, but you're the grate-est, in queso you didn't know!

What do you call a happy father?

A glad dad.

What do penguins do when they meet someone new?

They say something to break the ice.

What did the sand say to its dad?

"I shore do love you, Dad."

What did the stamp say to the envelope?

"I'm stuck on you."

Why did the kids give their dad a blanket for Father's Day?

Because they thought he was the coolest dad.

What happened when the two volcanoes met?

It was lava at first sight.

What did the little otter say to her dad?

"You're a father like no otter!"

Knock, knock.
Who's there?
Honeydew.
Honeydew who?
Honeydew you want a hug?

Why did the dad put sugar under his kid's pillow?

So they'd have sweet dreams.

Knock, knock.
Who's there?
Roach.
Roach who?
Roach you a letter—did you get it?

Knock, knock.
Who's there?
Spider.
Spider who?
In spider everything, I still love you.

What did the papa star say to the mama star?

"Isn't Junior bright?"

What did the bee say when it returned to the hive?

"Honey, I'm home!"

What did the baby light bulb say to its pop pop?

"I love you a watt."

Knock, knock.
Who's there?
Omelet.
Omelet who?
Omelet Dad sleep in on Father's Day.

What did the dad say when his daughter aced her oceanography project?

"Whale done!"

What did the baker's kid tell him on Father's Day?

"I would be muffin without you!"

What did the coffee mug say to its papa?

"I love you a latte!"

How is a baby bird like its dad?

It's a chirp off the old block.

When did the bee get married?

When he found his honey.

Kylee: Happy birthday, Nonno!

Nonno: Why did you give me a bunch of scrap paper?

Kylee: Because I love you to pieces!

What did one firefly say to her friend?

"You glow, girl!"

What did the atmosphere say to Earth?

"I've got you covered."

Knock, knock.
Who's there?
Tank.
Tank who?
Tank you for being my daddy!

Which season is the cutest?

Awww-*tumn.*

What do porcupines say when they hug?

"Ouch!"

What is the easiest way to get a squirrel to love you?

Act like a nut.

What did the tea leaves say to the cup of hot water?

"I can tell we're going to get oolong."

Last Laughs

What do you call a sleeping bull?

A bulldozer.

Cooper: Did you hear about the mouse that fell off a shelf into a soda?
Ava: Ouch!
Cooper: Don't worry—it was a soft drink.

Why did the penguin cross the road?

It was the chicken's day off.

Want to hear a long joke?

Joooooooooooooooooooooke!

Getting paid to sleep—now that would be my dream job.

Knock, knock.
Who's there?
Nose.
Nose who?
Nose any more good jokes?

If you found 20 bucks in your left pants pocket
and 50 in another, what would you have?

Somebody else's pants.

How does a monster count to 23?

On its fingers.

What does a giant say when he's bored?

"Fee-fi-ho-hum."

What did the zero say to the eight?

"Nice belt!"

Why did the superhero save the pickle?

So she could eat it later.

I invented a new word: *plagiarism.*

Father: Doctor, my son thinks he's a chicken!
Doctor: Why didn't you bring him to see me?
Father: I wanted to, but we need the eggs.

When can three buffalo hide under a small umbrella and not get wet?

When it's not raining.

What do you call a funny skunk?

Pun-gent.

Why did the two tall people get along so well?

They could really see eye to eye.

Idina: I'll call you later.
Dad: Don't call me later. Call me Dad!

What word is always spelled wrong in the dictionary?

Wrong.

Knock, knock.
Who's there?
Thor.
Thor who?
Thorry, wrong door.

What did the happy chocolate say to the cranky chocolate?

"Don't have a meltdown!"

Why did the dad carry the baby?

Because the baby can't carry the dad.

What time is it when a dinosaur sits on your watch?

Time to get a new watch.

What's worse than biting into an apple and finding a worm?

Biting into an apple and finding half a worm.

I went to buy a camouflage sweatshirt, but I couldn't find any.

What do you get when you drop a pumpkin?

Squash.

What did the Triceratops sit on?
Its tricera-bottom.

Why did the coach go to the bank?

To get his quarter back.

Fiona: Want to hear a story about a broken pencil?
Nora: No, thanks. I'm sure it has no point.

Knock, knock.
Who's there?
Olive.
Olive who?
Olive you, Daddio!

Mina: Does your puppy have a license?
Veda: No, she's not old enough to drive.

What do you call a can opener that doesn't work?

A can't opener.

What did they do at the Boston Tea Party?

I don't know—I wasn't invited.

Knock, knock.
Who's there?
Possum.
Possum who?
Possum food, please. I'm hungry!

What is the coldest month of the year?

Decem-brrrr.

Enzo: I went home and asked my dad for a pair of sneakers for gym.
Inez: What did he say?
Enzo: He said to tell Jim to buy his own sneakers.

Where do fathers keep their jokes?

In a dad-abase.

Why did the chicken stop crossing the road?

It was tired of the chicken jokes.

What's the difference between here and there?

The letter T.

Knock, knock.
Who's there?
Thistle.
Thistle who?
Thistle be the last joke in the book!